RICH 2F8 - 779 4864

☑ **W9-ADW-015**

THE

CONTEMPLATIVE

ROSARY

p. 5 Contemplative Prayer —

DAN BURKE and CONNIE ROSSINI

P. 5. Contemplation

THE
CONTEMPLATIVE
ROSARY

with St. John Paul II
and St. Teresa of Avila

EWTN PUBLISHING, INC.
Irondale, Alabama

Copyright © 2017 by Daniel Burke and Connie Rossini

Printed in the United States of America. All rights reserved.

Cover design by Coronation Media. Cover images: painting of John Paul II (2015), Emanuele Mazzoni / Alamy Stock Photo; José de Ribera, *Santa Teresa de Ávila* (1644), Heritage Image Partnership Ltd / Alamy Stock Photo.

Interior design by Perceptions Design Studio.

Except where otherwise noted, biblical references in this book are taken from the Catholic Edition of the Revised Standard Version of the Bible, copyright 1965, 1966 by the Division of Christian Education of the National Council of the Churches of Christ in the United States of America. Used by permission. All rights reserved.

English translation of the *Catechism of the Catholic Church* for the United States of America copyright © 1994, United States Catholic Conference, Inc.—Libreria Editrice Vaticana. English translation of the *Catechism of the Catholic Church*: Modifications from the Editio Typica copyright © 1997, United States Catholic Conference, Inc.—Libreria Editrice Vaticana.

Quotations from papal documents are from the Vatican website (w2.vatican.va) © Libreria Editrice Vaticana. All rights reserved. Used with permission.

Quotations from St. Teresa of Avila's *Way of Perfection* and *Interior Castle* are from *The Collected Works of St. Teresa of Avila*, Volume Two, translated by Kieran Kavanaugh and Otilio Rodriguez, copyright © 1980 by Washington Province of Discalced Carmelites, ICS Publications, 2131 Lincoln Road NE, Washington, DC 0002-1199, USA, www.icspublications.org.

No part of this book may be reproduced, stored in a retrieval system, or transmitted in any form, or by any means, electronic, mechanical, photocopying, or otherwise, without the prior written permission of the publisher, except by a reviewer, who may quote brief passages in a review.

EWTN Publishing, Inc., 817 Old Leeds Road, Irondale, AL 35210

Distributed by Sophia Institute Press, Box 5284, Manchester, NH 03108

Library of Congress Cataloging-in-Publication Data

Names: Burke, Dan, 1965- author.

Title: The contemplative rosary with St. John Paul II and St. Teresa of Avila / Dan Burke and Connie Rossini.

Description: Irondale, Alabama : EWTN Publishing, Inc., 2017. | Includes bibliographical references.

Identifiers: LCCN 2017025879 | ISBN 9781682780442 (pbk. : alk. paper)

Subjects: LCSH: Spiritual life—Catholic Church. | Contemplation. | Rosary. | Rosary—Meditations. | John Paul II, Pope, 1920-2005. | Teresa, of Avila, Saint, 1515-1582.

Classification: LCC BX2350.3 .B85 2017 | DDC 242/.74—dc23 LC record available at https://lccn.loc.gov/2017025879

Contents

Introduction

The Rosary as seen through the eyes of two contemplative Catholic saints will no doubt change your life. One of these saints, Teresa of Ávila, was a sixteenth-century Spanish nun and a Doctor of the Church. The other, Pope Saint John Paul II, was a twentieth-century philosopher, actor, and poet whom God chose to lead His Church in a powerful way that has led many to call him St. John Paul the Great.

Why was the contemplative life so important to them? What did contemplation mean to them? Saint John Paul tended to use the words *contemplative* and *contemplation* in a wider sense than Teresa did. For him, *contemplation* was often synonymous with *meditation*. But even *meditation* has a precise Catholic meaning that is different from the ways non-Catholics use the word. The *Catechism of the Catholic Church*, compiled during John Paul II's pontificate and under his direction, speaks of meditation in this way:

Meditation is above all a quest. The mind seeks to understand the why and how of the Christian life, in order to adhere and respond to what the Lord is asking. The required attentiveness is difficult to sustain. We are usually helped by books, and Christians do not want for them: the Sacred Scriptures, particularly the Gospels, holy icons, liturgical texts of the day or season, writings of the spiritual fathers, works of spirituality, the great book of creation, and that of history, the page on which the "today" of God is written.[1]

For Catholics, meditation is the act of thinking about or pondering. But it is not thinking about just anything. It is pondering the face of God in Christ. This reading and reflecting on sacred writings is not a mere intellectual exercise. It is a prayer. Saint John Paul writes in his apostolic letter *Rosarium Virginis Mariae* (*On the Most Holy Rosary*):

To look upon the face of Christ, to recognize its mystery amid the daily events and the sufferings of his human life, and then to grasp the divine splendor definitively revealed in the Risen Lord, seated

---

[1] *Catechism of the Catholic Church* (hereafter CCC), no. 2705.

in glory at the right hand of the Father; this is the task of every follower of Christ and therefore the task of each one of us.[2]

We can sum up the Pope's words in this way: The Christian's task is to:

- look upon the face of Christ
- see the mystery of the Incarnation in the details of His life
- recognize God's majesty, revealed in the risen and ascended Lord

John Paul II goes on to say:

In contemplating Christ's face, we become open to receiving the mystery of Trinitarian life, experiencing ever new the love of the Father and delighting in the joy of the Holy Spirit.[3]

Meditation begins with pondering, but it does not end there. It ends with standing in awe before the grandeur and mystery of God's quest for union with us. This adoration prepares the soul for a greater union with God, a union

---

[2] Saint John Paul II, Apostolic Letter *Rosarium Virginus Mariae* (hereafter *RVM*), October 16, 2002, no. 1.
[3] *RVM* 9.

that will be accomplished by God's drawing the soul into the realm of infused contemplation.

Catholics generally make distinctions between the mental prayer in which we speak from the heart and the vocal prayer that uses words written by others. Meditation is one form of mental prayer, but in this book, both Pope John Paul II and Saint Teresa will teach us how reflecting on the Gospel can enrich our vocal prayer. The Rosary is the prayer par excellence that unites vocal prayer and mental prayer in a way that can, by God's sacred action, lift our hearts to the heights of contemplation.

Saint Teresa of Avila said, "Mental prayer in my opinion is nothing else than a close sharing between friends; it means taking time frequently to be alone with him who we know loves us."[4] Saint Teresa did not write much about methods of meditation in her teaching on mental prayer. Her view was that plenty of people had already done so. Her audience — primarily cloistered Carmelite nuns — already knew how to meditate on Sacred Scripture. She speaks of prayer in simpler terms. It is "a close sharing between friends." The soul withdraws from its ordinary activities to spend time with the God who loves it.

---

[4] Saint Teresa of Ávila, *Life*, trans. E. Allison Peers, 8.5.

Saint Teresa focused the vast majority of her teaching on prayer on her understanding of contemplation. She defined contemplation as "a Divine union, in which the Lord takes His delight in the soul and the soul takes its delight in Him."[5] For her, the word *contemplation* denotes the final end of meditation. This type of contemplation is referred to as infused, because God "breathes" it into the soul. It is a sublime union with God in prayer that He brings about Himself. It is supernaturally initiated and deepened by God. We can prepare ourselves for contemplation through prayer and faithfulness to God's will throughout the day, but only God can draw us into the deepest waters of contemplation.

As a more formal definition of contemplation consistent with the teachings of Saint Teresa and fellow Doctor of the Church Saint John of the Cross, we can say that contemplative prayer is

an infused supernatural gift, that originates completely outside of our will or ability, by which a person becomes freely absorbed in God producing a real awareness, desire, and love for Him. This often gentle or delightful and sometimes non-sensible

---

[5] Saint Teresa of Avila, *The Way of Perfection* (hereafter WP), trans. Otilio Rodriguez and Kieran Kavanaugh (Washington, DC: ICS, 1980), chap. 16.

encounter can yield special insights into things of the spirit and results in a deeper and tangible desire to love God and neighbor in thought, word, and deed. It is important to note that infused contemplation is a state that can be prepared for, but cannot in any way be produced by the will or desire of a person through methods or ascetical practices.[6]

That is a quick overview of the teachings of Saints John Paul II and Teresa of Avila on contemplation. What, then, is the Contemplative Rosary?

In the Contemplative Rosary, we seek to transcend the rote recitation of prayers, which Jesus, as well as non-Catholics, might criticize as "vain repetition."[7] The Contemplative Rosary begins with a purposeful and devoted attention to Christ's presence in each mystery and every uttered prayer. This attention is only the first step, however. The focus is worship, drawing our hearts to bow in awe before the Triune God, whom the Rosary reveals to us. In the Contemplative Rosary, we place every moment of our lives before the throne of God, also recognizing the

---

[6] Daniel Burke and Fr. John Bartunek, *Navigating the Interior Life — Spiritual Direction and the Journey to God* (Steubenville, OH: Emmaus Road, 2012), glossary.

[7] See Matt. 6:7, King James Version.

mystery of the Incarnation at work within us. We place our bodies, minds, and hearts at the Lord's disposal. We long for the deeper union of infused contemplation. We yearn for Him without anxiety, waiting patiently for Him to come to us. If God wills, the Contemplative Rosary can be a meeting point with God, in which He rewards our contemplative disposition with the first taste of a deeper union with Him.

The Universal Call
to Contemplation

———————————◆———————————

At this point some may ask, "If the Contemplative Rosary is meant to prepare hearts for infused contemplation, is it really for ordinary Christians? Isn't infused contemplation for just a few chosen souls?"

For centuries, many Christians have wrongly thought infused contemplation was for others, not for them. Many have divided the Christian life into two camps — the active and the contemplative. Laypeople, they think, are called to an active life and cannot be expected to pray much because of their many duties. They must be content with ordinary ways of holiness; God does not intend the heights of prayer for them.

But is this what the Church teaches? On the contrary, the Church teaches that everyone is called to the heights of union with God. The Fathers of Vatican II wrote:

> Fortified by so many and such powerful means of salvation, all the faithful, whatever their condition or state, are called by the Lord, each in his own way, to that perfect holiness whereby the Father Himself is perfect.[8]

Yes, we are all called to perfect holiness! But only God can make us perfectly holy. He does this in and through the sacraments and infused contemplation.

Like the Church, Saint Teresa also teaches that laypeople can become contemplatives. In her letters, she counsels her businessman brother Lorenzo as God draws him into mystical prayer. She even speaks about contemplation in the context of teaching her Sisters about one of the prayers of the Rosary — the Our Father. In *The Way of Perfection*, she teaches them how to pray the Our Father in a way that leads far beyond empty repetition. Line by line, she reveals the deep and profound meaning of each petition and calls their hearts to engage a reality that is far beyond the basic text. For example, at the words, "Forgive us our trespasses, as we forgive those who trespass against us," she calls them to consider that the grace easily to forgive others comes

---

[8] Second Vatican Council, Dogmatic Constitution on the Church *Lumen Gentium*, November 21, 1964, no. 11.

only with infused contemplation in the prayer of union. Only when we are closely united to our Lord in contemplative union do we forgive in the manner that God calls us to forgive. Thus, according to Saint Teresa, the Our Father puts the petitions of contemplatives in our mouths. This is a prayer Jesus gave to all Christians, even the youngest and the least educated. If its petitions imply infused graces, we can say that the prayer itself implies that all Christians are called to contemplative union with Christ.[9]

Elsewhere Saint Teresa speaks plainly:

> The Lord invites us all; and since He is Truth Itself, we cannot doubt Him.... I feel sure that none will fail to receive this living water unless they cannot keep to the path.[10]

In *Rosarium Virginis Mariae* Saint John Paul II writes that contemplating the face of Christ is "the task of every follower of Christ."[11] In fact, this contemplation will be the chief joy of Heaven, when we truly see Christ face-to-face. Our life on earth is meant to prepare us for the life of Heaven. We ponder the face of Christ not only in

[9] See *WP* 36.
[10] Ibid., 19.
[11] *RVM* 1.

paintings, or in our imagination, or figuratively through reading the Gospels; as we mature in Christ, He brings the soul into His presence in an ever more frequent and growing union. In infused contemplation God draws us to look upon His face ever more fully.

The Contemplative Rosary is not just for those who have reached a high state of prayer. It is for everyone who desires to live a more contemplative life, a life centered on pondering the mysteries of our Faith and making ourselves more present to God, so that He may be more present to us.

Staying Close to Jesus

Saint Teresa, as we noted earlier, is best known for her teaching on mental prayer, especially in her two classics *The Way of Perfection* and *Interior Castle*. But she also taught about vocal prayer. *The Way of Perfection* discusses the meaning of the Our Father in chapters 24 through 42. Teresa explains what each petition of the Our Father teaches us about mental prayer and growth in virtue. She also instructs us on how to pray the Our Father and other vocal prayers as we should—with a heart oriented to God.

Let's look at several important principles she reveals.

First and most importantly she writes, "I want you to understand that it is good for you, if you are to recite the Our Father well, to remain at the side of the Master who taught this prayer to you."[12] Whether we practice mental prayer or vocal prayer, Jesus must always be our focus. It is

[12] WP 24.5.

not enough merely to assent to the idea that Jesus is our focus, but we must actually live the reality of Jesus being our focus. We pray not in order to get something out of God, but in order to come near to Him. Authentic prayer is an expression of the heart enflamed with love. We remain at the side of the Master when, instead of mindlessly reciting our prayers, we acknowledge His presence with us and yield to His work in us and for us. In the Contemplative Rosary, we do this as we gaze upon Him through the holy eyes of the Mother of God.

The Rosary provides us with an easy way to keep Jesus at our side as we pray. It was designed for this very purpose, to help ordinary Catholics meditate on the life of Christ, drawing their hearts to worship Him. The Rosary gives us twenty mysteries to meditate on, twenty themes on which to focus our minds, hearts, and imaginations—twenty paths to lead our hearts to Heaven.

Although Marian in character, the Rosary is nonetheless focused on Christ. In fact, it is with Mary and led by her that we come to see the face of Christ in a way we could never achieve on our own. Saint John Paul II wrote:

> Mary constantly sets before the faithful the "mysteries" of her Son, with the desire that the contemplation of those mysteries will release all their saving

power. In the recitation of the Rosary, the Christian community enters into contact with the memories and the contemplative gaze of Mary.[13]

In the Rosary, we ponder with Mary those things she "pondered in her heart" in the Gospels.[14] Her memories are the memories of the Incarnation. She is always thinking about her Son. When we look upon her, she turns our gaze to her Son.

Saint John Paul II tells us that we must go beyond learning about Christ's teachings. We must learn Christ Himself. In the Rosary, we enter "the school of Mary." We sit at her feet as she shares the stories so close to her heart. She teaches us, as she taught the servants at the Wedding of Cana, to "do whatever He tells us."[15]

---

[13] RVM 11.
[14] See Luke 2:19.
[15] See RVM 14.

Attention and Distractions

———————◆———————

In her instruction on the Our Father, Saint Teresa tells her Sisters that true prayer requires solitude. Jesus exemplified this in the Gospels, when He went aside by Himself to pray.[16] We may scratch our heads at Saint Teresa's teaching, since she is speaking particularly about vocal prayer. Wasn't the Our Father meant to be said aloud? Don't we often pray the Rosary as a family or a parish community? How can we pray it together and yet be alone?

Solitude in prayer goes beyond entering our room by ourselves and closing the door.[17] If all we do is place ourselves physically apart from other people, we do not have the type of solitude Saint Teresa encourages. God invites us, out of His desire to commune with us, to set

[16] WP 24.4–5; see also Matt. 14:23; 26:36; Mark 1:35; 6:36; 14:32; Luke 5:16; 6:12.
[17] See Matt. 6:6.

aside anything that would distract us from this encounter of love. We should not have divided hearts, as if we are listening to another conversation while we are speaking to our Lord. This kind of attention falls short of what is necessary to allow us to receive all that He desires to give us in prayer.

When we pray the Rosary, whether alone or with others, we deliberately set aside worldly matters. We pursue an atmosphere, both internally and externally, that is proper to prayer. If we are at home, this means turning off and setting aside any electronic media or anything that produces background noise or buzzing in our pockets or purses. In church, this means discouraging chatter. We set aside a special time and place in which nothing is happening but prayer.

But exterior solitude is only the beginning. We also cultivate solitude in our hearts. Interior solitude presents a greater challenge. We consciously put aside our daydreams, plans, and all reflections that have nothing to do with our prayer. We make a quiet place in our hearts where we can be alone with Jesus, even if we are in a room with other people. This takes both vigilance and practice.

Note that we do not seek to be absolutely alone, even in our hearts. We seek to be alone *with God*. We do not set aside all thoughts as taught in non-Christian Eastern religions, but only those thoughts that would distract us from Him. Saint John Paul II notes that although the Rosary is a form of meditation, it differs from non-Christian meditation techniques. It is not "aimed at attaining a high level of spiritual concentration" (or, we might add, an altered state of consciousness), nor should we think of the rosary beads as somehow magical, like an amulet. The Rosary is not an end in itself. Rather, it is a means of contemplating Christ. Like the Eastern Christian "Jesus Prayer," the Rosary can satisfy the desire for a repetitive, meditative form of prayer but in an authentically Christian manner.[18]

In *Interior Castle*, Saint Teresa writes bluntly about the importance of attention during prayer:

> A prayer in which a person is not aware of whom he is speaking to, what he is asking, who it is who is asking and of whom, I do not call prayer, however much the lips move.[19]

When vocal prayers are prayed with attention and devotion, they rise to the level of mental prayer that simply uses words composed by someone else. Teresa anticipated

[18] RVM 28.

[19] Saint Teresa of Avila, *Interior Castle* (hereafter IC), trans. Otilio Rodriguez and Kieran Kavanaugh (Washington, DC: ICS, 1980), 1.1.7.

that some of her nuns would protest against engaging their minds in vocal prayer. "You're asking us to practice mental prayer, and we can't do that!" She writes:

> You are right in saying that this vocal prayer is now in fact mental prayer. But I tell you that surely I don't know how mental prayer can be separated from vocal prayer if the vocal prayer is to be recited well with the understanding of whom we are speaking to. It is even an obligation that we strive to pray with attention.[20]

Many of us learned the Rosary as children. If we were not taught to pray it well with attention, or we have formed bad habits of laziness in thought, it will take effort to begin collecting our thoughts to focus our minds and hearts on Jesus, as Saint Teresa says we should. She calls this practice *recollection*.

Helping Catholics to overcome these difficulties was one of the chief goals of Saint John Paul II's encyclical *Rosarium Virginis Mariae*. He wished to revitalize the Rosary, to illuminate its riches, to wake us out of our stupor of "vain repetition," and to help us realize what a precious gift the Church gives us in this prayer. Attention and devotion

---

[20] Ibid., 24.6.

hold the secret to drawing ourselves, and allowing God to draw us, ever more deeply into the powerful mysteries of the Rosary and into contemplative prayer. Saint John Paul II quotes his predecessor Blessed Paul VI:

> Without contemplation, the Rosary is a body without soul, and its recitation runs the risk of becoming a mechanical repetition of formulas, in violation of the admonition of Christ: "In praying do not heap up empty phrases as the Gentiles do; for they think they will be heard for their many words."[21]

Above all, this mystic saint desired that the Rosary, which he saw as a "compendium of the Gospel," draw us into the mystery of the Incarnation.[22]

But what do we do when our minds are distracted? How can we cultivate the attention that changes "empty phrases" into heavenly communion with the Blessed Trinity? Even Saint Teresa had trouble concentrating during prayer. In fact, she is well known to have spent years struggling with interior distractions.

Saint Teresa encourages us by acknowledging that there will be some days when we truly cannot help our

[21] RVM 12, quoting *Marialis Cultus* 156 and Matt. 6:7.
[22] Ibid., 19.

distractions. She mentions times of sickness, weak constitutions, and harassment by the devil. A mother who has been up all night with an infant or a sick child might also be unable to overcome distractions. So might a person enduring trials at work or in his personal life that keep his thoughts whirling, no matter how much effort he puts into managing them. If we are truly striving to focus on Christ, rather than just being lazy in our prayer, Saint Teresa counsels us not to worry about distractions and difficulties. Worrying will only make them worse. We must do the best we can and most of all simply show up every day to be with God in prayer.

Even so, it is incumbent upon us to make a genuine effort to overcome distractions.[23] There are many adjustments we can make to improve our time in prayer. We can avoid engaging in activities just before our prayer time that we know tend to distract us—such as spending too much time watching TV or with digital media. We should always endeavor to get adequate sleep so that we can be alert for prayer. Efforts to pray well often begin before our set time of prayer. They extend to the choices we make throughout our day.

Saint Teresa gives practical suggestions for those with distracted minds. "The best remedy I find is to strive to

[23] WP 24.5.

center the mind upon the one to whom the words are addressed.... Represent the Lord Himself as close to you, and behold how lovingly and humbly He is teaching you.... I'm not asking you to do anything more than look at Him."[24]

In other words, people who find it very difficult to engage their minds in thinking about the mysteries of the Incarnation can practice recollection in another way. Instead of using their intellect, they can use their imagination.

Some people find it helpful to look at a picture during prayer. Saint Teresa recommends this as one possible method of meditation.[25] With the Rosary prayers later in this book you will find carefully chosen paintings to represent the Mysteries of the Rosary. Gazing on these paintings can help a distracted mind to focus. When we do not have an exterior image available, we can also use our imaginations to recall a favorite painting or scene from the Gospels. When we find that our intellect is out of control, we can worship Christ with our imagination. Focusing on an image, whether exterior or interior, helps calm whirling thoughts. It can be a great aid to those who have developed habits of wandering thoughts during prayer. Some people will be astonished and relieved by how well this works for them.

[24] Ibid., 24.6; 26.1, 3.
[25] Ibid., 26.9.

Saint Teresa also recommends praying with books that have reflections in them.[26] We hope this book will help here too. For each decade of the Rosary, we offer meditations and a particular method to help focus your intellect and your will on Christ.

[26] WP 26.10.

Vocal Prayer and Mental Prayer

———————◆———————

Saint Teresa writes, "I tell you that it is very possible that while you are reciting the Our Father or some other vocal prayer, the Lord may raise you to perfect contemplation."[27] This follows logically from what we revealed earlier through this great saint: vocal prayer done well is simply mental prayer using words composed by someone else. Vocal prayer of this caliber can be as helpful to one's spiritual life as mental prayer because it *is* mental prayer.

Does that mean that vocal prayer is enough? If we pray the Contemplative Rosary daily, can we skip daily mental prayer? Or do we have to spend time praying from the heart as well?

[27] *W/P* 25.

This is an important question for Catholics, especially lifelong Catholics. Most of us learned vocal prayers from our parents or teachers. We were taught the Rosary, the Guardian Angel Prayer, and the Table Blessing. If we were lucky, we might have learned how to recite a morning offering or make a daily examination of conscience as well. But very few of us were taught how to practice mental prayer. We feel embarrassed or tongue-tied when we try to speak to God from our hearts. What are we supposed to say? Unless someone instructs us as adults, our mental prayer is likely to be a rambling monologue about our day or a list of petitions. It's no wonder that so few of us find joy in this type of prayer or persevere in it.

The Contemplative Rosary can help us here. Simply put, we should not pray the Rosary instead of spending time in mental prayer alone. Instead, the Contemplative Rosary teaches us how to meditate on the powerful images and truths revealed by the Holy Spirit in Sacred Scripture, so that we can then employ a similar meditation in our time of mental prayer. Such meditation is a favorite mental prayer of the saints.

The Contemplative Rosary can transform both our vocal prayer and our mental prayer.

As we learn to focus our minds, hearts, and imaginations on Christ while we "tell our beads" (as Christians used to say), we can cross over to doing this without the anchor of the Rosary prayers. Our vocal prayer and mental prayer thus become one, helping us to carry on the same conversation with Christ throughout the day, in different forms.

When we devote ourselves to praying the Rosary well, a surprising temptation may arise: to multiply our Rosaries. If five decades a day are good, aren't twenty so much better? And why stop there? Why not say the whole Rosary several times each day?

Saint Teresa, the great mystic and spiritual director, would commend our enthusiasm for prayer but then prudently advise us to limit our vocal prayers. One practical reason for this is that when we oblige ourselves to say the Rosary several times a day, it can become an item to check off our to-do list. We lose that first enthusiasm by overdoing it. We also have limited time for prayer during most of our lives. More time spent in vocal prayer usually means less time for dedicated mental prayer (and for doing our duty well). Saint Teresa writes that some people

> are so fond of speaking and of reciting many vocal prayers very quickly like one who wants to get a job done, since they oblige themselves to recite these every day, that even though, as I say, the Lord places

His Kingdom in their hands, they do not receive it. But with their vocal prayers they think they are doing better and they distract themselves from the prayer of quiet.[28]

Saint Teresa is speaking here of those experiencing an early form of infused contemplation. She is saying that when we have too many vocal prayers to say, our goal easily changes to getting them done instead of praying them well. They become less, rather than more, contemplative. The Holy Spirit might be moving us to linger silently on the meditation of a mystery, but we feel that we can't stop or we will never fit all our prayers in. So we find ourselves working against the Holy Spirit. God may even give us the first taste of infused contemplation while we are praying the Rosary, but in our hurry to meet self-imposed goals, we ignore His call to union and fill the space with words. We forget that the very purpose of prayer is communing with the Lord. We are tempted toward the vain repetition the Gospel condemns. In the end, it is better to pray one decade of the Rosary well than to spend hours praying the Rosary in a manner that reflects only minimal engagement of our hearts with God.

[28] WP 30.

An important practice to protect ourselves from saying no to God when He draws us deeper into prayer through the Rosary is to pause when we are drawn into the mystery. Said another way, whenever we are struck or moved by an idea, thought, or insight related to our prayer of the Rosary, we should pause for a moment and allow God's work in our hearts and minds to soak in. Once the moment is passed we can gently return to our prayer. This approach will help to condition us to be responsive with a yes to God when He meets us in prayer in a deeper way.

As a norm, vocal prayer should supplement our dedicated time in mental prayer and help us to remain in God's presence throughout the day. It is not an end in itself; in fact, if we pray it the way the Holy Spirit desires, it will be the beginning of a profound prayer journey to union with the Blessed Trinity.

To learn more about mental prayer we recommend *Into the Deep — Finding Peace through Prayer*, which presents, in a very simple and concise way, the path that will allow you to discover Jesus and to draw near to Him in prayer.[29]

---

[29] To learn more about this book and about mental prayer go to SpiritualDirection.com/pray, where you will also find a free mini-course on mental prayer. Use the code DISCOVER to access the course.

The Contemplative
Rosary Method

———————— ◆ ————————

In this section, we give you a general outline of the Contemplative Rosary method. In the section that follows, we will provide specific meditations and other elements for each of the mysteries that you can use while you pray the Rosary using the method.

Throughout the centuries, there have been many variations of the Rosary as Christians adapted it to fit particular situations. In *Rosarium Virginis Mariae*, Saint John Paul II proposed a renewed way of praying the Rosary, but he did not insist that everyone should use this new way. Instead, he desired to revitalize the Rosary for a new generation.

Keep in mind this wise saying of Saint Teresa: "Do that which best stirs you to love."[30] If you have a favorite

---

[30] *IC* 4.1.7.

practice that helps make your recitation of the Rosary more contemplative, do not think you must change it just because Saint John Paul II gave different suggestions or because the meditations we offer in this book are different from the ones you have used before. Sometimes we need a slight change in our prayer practice in order to help us refocus and grow. But other times, when we are on a proven and fruitful path, we need to remain on that path. There are few hard-and-fast rules about praying the Rosary. Follow the general guidance for making vocal prayer more contemplative that we laid out previously. The specific practices you use are of lesser importance. These specifics are meant to facilitate your Contemplative Rosary, not to bind you permanently to one set of meditations or a select group of paintings.

OPENING PRAYERS

One good custom is to begin the Rosary with the Apostles' Creed, then an Our Father and three Hail Marys for the intentions of the Pope as a way of orienting our hearts to the universal and ecclesial nature of the Rosary. Saint John Paul II writes that the opening words of Psalm 70: "O God, come to my [assistance]; O Lord, make haste to help me," might be prayed at the beginning of the Rosary instead, indicating our need of God's help in order to pray worthily.[31] This verse is recited at the beginning of Morning and Evening Prayer by those who pray the Liturgy of the Hours. It thus connects the Rosary more closely with the official prayers of the Church.

THE MYSTERIES

Saint John Paul II encourages the use of icons or other representations of each mystery. As Saint Teresa suggests, using our senses or imagination helps to keep our otherwise distracted minds on God. Jesus Himself is an icon, an image of the invisible God. Therefore, it is fitting to use images to help us come closer to Him.[32]

Many people, especially when they pray the Rosary in a group, are used to reading a short passage from Scripture after each mystery is announced. The Pope encourages us to practice this whenever we pray the Rosary. Doing so makes Sacred Scripture a vital part of the Rosary, connecting this prayer to the Liturgy and to our own time of mental prayer, when we meditate only on the sacred text. It reminds us that prayer is not only about speaking to God, but also

[31] *RVM* 37.
[32] Ibid., 29.

about listening to Him. We listen to His Word and then respond to it as we say the prayers for each mystery. The reading can be long or short, and even accompanied by a short homily in solemn celebrations.[33] After this proclamation of the Word, a short silence is fitting.[34]

Saint John Paul II also proposed another set of mysteries that many of us are now familiar with: the Mysteries of Light (Luminous Mysteries). These scenes from the Gospels fill in the gap between Christ's childhood and His Passion with events from His public ministry. The Mysteries of Light are: the Baptism of the Lord, the Wedding at Cana, the Proclamation of the Kingdom, the Transfiguration, and the Institution of the Eucharist. They have a distinctly sacramental character not found in the traditional fifteen mysteries. They remind us that our salvation is revealed not just in Jesus' life two thousand years ago, but also in Baptism, Matrimony, the Eucharist, and the other sacraments. The Pope notes that only the second of these mysteries explicitly mentions Mary. Yet the instruction she gives to the servants at the Wedding at Cana "becomes the great maternal counsel which Mary addresses to the Church of every age: 'Do whatever He tells you'" (John

[33] Ibid., 30.
[34] Ibid., 31.

2:5). Her words form the foundation of this entire group of mysteries.[35]

OUR FATHER

Jesus came to lead us to God the Father. It is therefore right for us to begin each decade by addressing God as Our Father. He is the Father of Jesus and, through Jesus, the Father of all of us. The Our Father reminds us that we are part of God's family, in communion with one another, even when we pray the Rosary alone.[36]

Studying Saint Teresa's exposition of the Our Father in chapters 24 through 42 of *The Way of Perfection* would be an excellent means of enriching our prayer.

HAIL MARY

The Hail Mary is the central prayer of the Rosary. If we pray the entire Rosary according to the new form offered by Saint John Paul II, we say the Hail Mary two hundred times. How can we pray this prayer in a more contemplative manner?

[35] *RVM* 21.
[36] Ibid., 32.

Saint John Paul II calls the Hail Marys the threads over which the mysteries of the Rosary are woven. They present to us in miniature the mystery of the God-Man, the same mystery presented to us on a larger scale throughout the Rosary.[37] The Hail Mary is a profoundly Christ-centered prayer. Rather than taking our eyes off Christ, it focuses our attention on Him. It begins with the greeting of the Angel Gabriel at the Annunciation, coupled with the words of Saint Elizabeth at the Visitation. It ends with our supplication for Mary's maternal care for us and our loved ones, in light of our union with her divine Son. It calls us to share in God's delight in the Incarnation. We contemplate the Incarnation with God Himself. Just as in the Creation He pronounced the world *good*, so God stood back in delight at the conception of His eternal Son in the womb of the Virgin. "The repetition of the Hail Mary in the Rosary gives us a share in God's own wonder and pleasure: in jubilant amazement we acknowledge the greatest miracle of history."[38] This repetition is also like a sentence of love spoken repeatedly to one's beloved.[39]

[37] *RVM* 18.
[38] Ibid., 33.
[39] Ibid., 26.

In *Marialis Cultus*, Blessed Paul VI noted the custom of adding, after the name of Jesus, a brief statement of faith related to the mystery we are reflecting on, such as "who was conceived in you by the Holy Spirit" while meditating on the Annunciation. Saint John Paul II encourages us to take up this custom. He says that Jesus' name is "the center of gravity" of the entire prayer, the hinge that links the two halves of the Hail Mary. Instead of mumbling the name of Jesus, as sometimes happens, we should highlight it by adding a statement that makes us pay attention. This helps us to engage with our prayer rather than just "say our prayers." It pulls our wandering minds back to Christ and anchors them in the mystery we seek to explore.[40]

GLORY BE

Adoration of the Trinity, says Saint John Paul II, is the goal of prayer. He notes that the Glory Be, "the high-point of contemplation, [should] be given due prominence in the Rosary." In public celebrations, we should sing it. The Glory Be transports us to Mount Tabor, the site of the Transfiguration, where we can say with St. Peter, "It is well

[40] Ibid., 33.

that we are here!"[41] It's so easy to overlook this short prayer, making it an afterthought. However, the Incarnation we ponder in the Rosary took place so that we could worship the Holy Trinity in purity of spirit. Perhaps we should linger here a moment in silence, rather than rushing on to the next prayer.

The Church asks us to bow when we pray the Glory Be during the Liturgy of the Hours. Bowing when we pray the Glory Be in the Rosary can be another reminder of the importance of this prayer and a physical reverence that provides another aid to our desire to be fully engaged as we pray.

CONCLUDING PRAYER
FOR EACH MYSTERY

Many of us recite the Fatima Prayer after the Glory Be: "O my Jesus, forgive us our sins, save us from the fires of Hell, lead all souls to Heaven, especially those in most need of Thy mercy."[42] Saint John Paul II encourages us

---

[41] *RVM* 34; Luke 9:33.

[42] The Fatima Prayer, or Decade Prayer, was added by the Blessed Mother at Fatima, Portugal, in 1917, in one of the apparitions to three young shepherd children, Lucia dos Santos and Saints Jacinta and Francisco Marto.

to say a concluding prayer asking for the grace to imitate the mystery we have just finished praying. This helps us to connect the Rosary with our daily lives.[43] We include short concluding prayers in this book that can be used for this purpose.

CLOSING PRAYER

Either beginning or concluding the Rosary with prayers for the Pope highlights again that the Rosary is a prayer not just for the individual, but for building up the whole Church. The soul may now want to "burst forth" into the Salve Regina or the Litany of Loreto. Saint John Paul II encourages us to indulge this desire.[44]

[43] *RVM* 35.
[44] *RVM* 37.

How to Pray the Rosary

———————— ◆ ————————

The Rosary consists of five decades of Hail Marys. As we pray each decade, we reflect on one mystery—an event in the life of Jesus or Mary. There are four sets of mysteries: the Joyful Mysteries (usually prayed on Mondays and Saturdays), the Luminous Mysteries (usually prayed on Thursdays), the Sorrowful Mysteries (usually prayed on Tuesdays and Fridays), and the Glorious Mysteries (usually prayed on Sundays and Wednesdays).

The Joyful Mysteries
1. The Annunciation
2. The Visitation
3. The Nativity
4. The Presentation
5. The Finding of the Child Jesus in the Temple

The Luminous Mysteries
   1. The Baptism of Christ in the Jordan
   2. The Wedding Feast at Cana
   3. The Proclamation of the Kingdom
   4. The Transfiguration of Jesus
   5. The Institution of the Eucharist

The Sorrowful Mysteries
   1. The Agony in the Garden
   2. The Scourging at the Pillar
   3. The Crowning with Thorns
   4. The Carrying of the Cross
   5. The Crucifixion

The Glorious Mysteries
   1. The Resurrection
   2. The Ascension
   3. The Descent of the Holy Spirit
   4. The Assumption of Mary
   5. The Coronation of Mary

HOW TO PRAY THE CONTEMPLATIVE ROSARY

1 Sign of the Cross, prayers for the intentions of the Pope, and the Apostles' Creed
or Sign of the Cross and Psalm 70:1

2 Our Father

3 Three Hail Marys

4 Glory Be

5 Announce the first mystery, read a relevant Scripture passage, pause for a few moments of silence. Then pray the Our Father, ten Hail Marys (one for each bead, adding the suggested clause or one of your own after the name of Jesus, while meditating on the First Mystery), a Glory Be, the Fatima Prayer, and the Concluding Prayer.

6-9 Repeat the sequence for the remaining decades, meditating on the Second, Third, Fourth, and Fifth Mysteries.

10 Pray the Hail, Holy Queen, the Concluding Prayer, and the Saint Michael Prayer (optional), and the Sign of the Cross.

The Order of Prayers

Opening Prayers

> *As you hold the Crucifix:*
>> Sign of the Cross
>> Prayers for the intentions of the Pope[45]
>> Apostles' Creed
>
>> *or:*
>> Sign of the Cross
>> Psalm 70:1
>
> First bead: Our Father
> Next three beads: three Hail Marys
> Glory Be

For Each Mystery

Announce the first mystery and read a relevant Scripture passage slowly with attention. Even if you are alone, it is good to read the passage out loud. Pause for a few moments of silence. Then recite the following prayers while meditating on that mystery:

[45] You may also make prayer requests at the beginning of the Rosary or at the beginning of each decade, or offer each Hail Mary for a specific person.

Our Father

Ten Hail Marys (adding the suggested clause or one of your own after the name of Jesus)

Glory Be

Fatima Prayer

Concluding Prayer

Repeat for each mystery.

You do not need to announce the fruit of each mystery unless you wish to. The concluding prayers also focus on these fruits.

Each mystery is paired with a painting we chose for its ability to draw the observer into the mystery. You may want to imagine yourself as one of the people in the painting, or standing next to them.

Each mystery also includes reflections that you can use in place of the paintings to keep your mind on Christ. Instead of trying to read through them all, linger on one meditation as long as it bears fruit.

If you are praying the Rosary by yourself and at any moment feel drawn to sit quietly in God's presence, obey that impulse until the feeling passes.

Conclude the Rosary with the Hail, Holy Queen and the Sign of the Cross. Many people add the Concluding Prayer and the Saint Michael Prayer after the Hail, Holy Queen.

PRAYERS OF THE ROSARY

Sign of the Cross

In the name of the Father, and of the Son and of the Holy Spirit. Amen.

Apostles' Creed

I believe in God, the Father Almighty, Creator of Heaven and earth; and in Jesus Christ, His only Son, our Lord, who was conceived by the Holy Spirit, born of the Virgin Mary, suffered under Pontius Pilate, was crucified, died, and was buried; He descended into Hell; the third day He rose again from the dead; He ascended into Heaven, and sits at the right hand of God, the Father Almighty; from thence He shall come to judge the living and the dead. I believe in the Holy Spirit, the holy Catholic Church, the communion of saints, the forgiveness of sins, the resurrection of the body, and life everlasting. Amen.

Our Father

Our Father, who art in Heaven, hallowed be Thy Name. Thy Kingdom come. Thy will be done, on earth as it is in Heaven. Give us this day our daily bread. And forgive us our trespasses, as we forgive those who trespass against us. And lead us not into temptation, but deliver us from evil. Amen.

Hail Mary

Hail Mary, full of grace, the Lord is with thee. Blessed art thou among women, and blessed is the fruit of thy womb, Jesus. Holy Mary, Mother of God, pray for us sinners, now and at the hour of our death. Amen.

Glory Be

(Head bowed) Glory Be to the Father, and to the Son, and to the Holy Spirit. As it was in the beginning, is now, and ever shall be, world without end. Amen.

Psalm 70:1

"O God, come to my assistance; O Lord, make haste to help me."

Fatima Prayer

O my Jesus, forgive us our sins, save us from the fires of Hell, lead all souls to Heaven, especially those who are most in need of Thy mercy.

Hail, Holy Queen

Hail, Holy Queen, Mother of Mercy! Our life, our sweetness, and our hope! To Thee do we cry, poor banished children of Eve; to Thee do we send up our sighs, mourning, and weeping in this valley of tears. Turn, then, most gracious advocate, thine eyes of mercy toward us, and after this our exile, show unto us the blessed fruit of thy womb, Jesus. O clement, O loving, O sweet Virgin Mary.

V. Pray for us, O Holy Mother of God.

R. That we may be made worthy of the promises of Christ.

Concluding Prayer

Let us pray. O God, whose only-begotten Son, by His life, death, and Resurrection, has purchased for us the rewards of eternal life, grant, we beseech Thee, that meditating upon these mysteries of the most Holy Rosary of the Blessed Virgin Mary, we may imitate what they contain, and obtain what they promise. Through the same Christ, our Lord. Amen.

Saint Michael Prayer

Saint Michael the Archangel, defend us in battle. Be our protection against the wickedness and snares of the devil. May God rebuke him, we humbly pray; and do thou, O prince of the heavenly host, by the power of God, cast into Hell Satan and all the evil spirits who roam throughout the world seeking the ruin of souls. Amen.

THE

CONTEMPLATIVE

ROSARY

◆

SCRIPTURE AND
REFLECTIONS

THE ANNUNCIATION

The Angel Gabriel announces the Incarnation to Mary.

FRUIT OF THE MYSTERY: HUMILITY

Scripture for Meditation
LUKE 1:26–38

In the sixth month the angel Gabriel was sent from God to a city of Galilee named Nazareth, to a virgin betrothed to a man whose name was Joseph, of the house of David; and the virgin's name was Mary. And he came to her and said, "Hail, full of grace, the Lord is with you!"

But she was greatly troubled at the saying, and considered in her mind what sort of greeting this might be. And the angel said to her, "Do not be afraid, Mary, for you have found favor with God. And behold, you will conceive in your womb and bear a son, and you shall call his name Jesus. He will be great, and will be called the Son of the Most High; and the Lord God will give to him the throne of his father

David, and he will reign over the house of Jacob for ever; and of his kingdom there will be no end."

And Mary said to the angel, "How can this be, since I have no husband?" And the angel said to her, "The Holy Spirit will come upon you, and the power of the Most High will overshadow you; therefore the child to be born will be called holy, the Son of God. And behold, your kinswoman Elizabeth in her old age has also conceived a son; and this is the sixth month with her who was called barren. For with God nothing will be impossible."

And Mary said, "Behold, I am the handmaid of the Lord; let it be to me according to your word." And the angel departed from her.

HAIL MARY, full of grace, the Lord is with thee. Blessed art thou among women, and blessed is the fruit of thy womb, Jesus, *who was conceived in you by the Holy Spirit*. Holy Mary, Mother of God, pray for us sinners, now and at the hour of our death. Amen.

REFLECTIONS

- Salvation history culminates in Gabriel's greeting, "an invitation to messianic joy: 'Rejoice, Mary'" (*RVM* 20).

- "The knot of Eve's disobedience was untied by Mary's obedience: what the virgin Eve bound through her disbelief, Mary loosened by her faith" (CCC 494).
- Mary's humble and unreserved yes "in the name of all human nature" is the ultimate example of what it means to say yes to God (see CCC 511).
- At this moment, the Word becomes flesh, a tiny embryo in Mary's womb.
- God lowered Himself to become an embryo. Thus, we raise ourselves above God when we refuse service that is "beneath us."
- As with Mary, certain souls' salvation depends on our yes to God's call to holiness and evangelization.
- Mary says yes to God without knowing what will happen and how it all will end. Our yes should not be contingent on our understanding or approval of God's plan.

CONCLUDING PRAYER

Pray for us, Mary, cause of our joy,
That we may follow God's will in perfect humility.

THE VISITATION

Mary visits her cousin Elizabeth.

FRUIT OF THE MYSTERY: LOVE OF NEIGHBOR

SCRIPTURE FOR MEDITATION
LUKE 1:39–50

In those days Mary arose and went with haste into the hill country, to a city of Judah, and she entered the house of Zechariah and greeted Elizabeth. And when Elizabeth heard the greeting of Mary, the babe leaped in her womb; and Elizabeth was filled with the Holy Spirit and she exclaimed with a loud cry, "Blessed are you among women, and blessed is the fruit of your womb! And why is this granted me, that the mother of my Lord should come to me? For behold, when the voice of your greeting came to my ears, the babe in my womb leaped for joy. And blessed is she who believed that there would be a fulfilment of what was spoken to her from the Lord." And Mary said, "My soul magnifies the Lord, and my spirit rejoices in God my Savior, for he has regarded the low estate of his hand-maiden. For behold, henceforth all generations will call me blessed; for he who is mighty has done great things for me, and holy is his name. And his mercy is on those who fear him from generation to generation."

HAIL MARY, full of grace, the Lord is with thee. Blessed art thou among women, and blessed is the fruit of thy womb, Jesus, *whom you carried to Elizabeth.* Holy Mary, Mother of God, pray for us sinners, now and at the hour of our death. Amen.

REFLECTIONS

- It is in Mary's nature to say yes to the needs of those around her. She will be quick to say yes when we are in need.
- Mary will bring Jesus to us and to others if we will but ask.
- Christ is central but hidden in these scenes, as He often is in our lives.
- Mary's first Christian apostolate was doing seemingly insignificant household chores at the service of others. Much of our Christian lives consists in small, hidden acts of love.

- Mary's canticle, the Magnificat in Luke 1:46–56, presents God's priorities in stark contrast to the way our world thinks. When life seems unfair, it is important to realize that God's ways are not our ways.
- John the Baptist leaps for joy at the sound of Mary's voice and at the presence of Christ (see *RVM* 20).
- Elizabeth calls the unborn Jesus "Lord" (and John the Baptist witnesses to Him) at the beginning of Mary's pregnancy.

CONCLUDING PRAYER

Pray for us, Mary, cause of our joy,
That we may love our neighbors and bring Christ into their lives.

THE NATIVITY

Jesus is born in Bethlehem.

FRUIT OF THE MYSTERY: POVERTY OF SPIRIT

SCRIPTURE FOR MEDITATION
LUKE 2:4–17

And Joseph also went up from Galilee, from the city of Nazareth, to Judea, to the city of David, which is called Bethlehem, because he was of the house and lineage of David, to be enrolled with Mary, his betrothed, who was with child. And while they were there, the time came for her to be delivered. And she gave birth to her first-born son and wrapped him in swaddling cloths, and laid him in a manger, because there was no place for them in the inn.

And in that region there were shepherds out in the field, keeping watch over their flock by night. And an angel of the Lord appeared to them, and the glory of the Lord shone around them, and they were filled with fear. And the angel said to them, "Be not afraid; for behold, I bring you good news of a great joy which will come to all the people; for to you is born this day in the city of David a Savior, who is Christ the Lord. And this will be a sign for you: you will find a babe wrapped in swaddling cloths and lying in a manger." And suddenly there was with the angel a multitude of the heavenly host praising God and saying, "Glory to God in the highest, and on earth peace among men with whom he is pleased!"

When the angels went away from them into heaven, the shepherds said to one another, "Let us go over to Bethlehem and see this thing that has happened, which the Lord has made known to us." And they went with haste, and found Mary and Joseph, and the babe lying in a manger. And when they saw it they made known the saying which had been told them concerning this child.

HAIL MARY, full of grace, the Lord is with thee. Blessed art thou among women, and blessed is the fruit of thy womb, Jesus, *who was born to you in Bethlehem*. Holy Mary, Mother of God, pray for us sinners, now and at the hour of our death. Amen.

REFLECTIONS

- The all-powerful God condescended to the weakness and smallness of a helpless baby to redeem us from the bondage of sin.

- The innkeeper could have been transformed by saying yes to Christ. How often do we refuse Him in our lives because we are too busy or have other *important* things to tend to?
- What are the consequences of our no—our refusal to give God all that we are and all that we aspire to in this life?
- The angels shared the good news first with those who were lowly and despised.
- We can count on God's answers to our prayers, but often in unexpected ways—a stable instead of a room.
- The Wise Men demonstrated extraordinary effort to give their best to God. Do we give Him our best time, best efforts, best talents—or just what is left over?
- The angels sang, "Glory to God in the highest!" We echo their words at every Sunday Mass and at the end of each decade of the Rosary.

CONCLUDING PRAYER

Pray for us, Mary, cause of our joy,
That out of love for Christ we may detach our hearts from material things and the esteem of the world.

THE PRESENTATION

Jesus is presented in the Temple.

FRUIT OF THE MYSTERY: OBEDIENCE

SCRIPTURE FOR MEDITATION
LUKE 2:22–35

And when the time came for their purification according to the law of Moses, they brought him up to Jerusalem to present him to the Lord (as it is written in the law of the Lord, "Every male that opens the womb shall be called holy to the Lord") and to offer a sacrifice according to what is said in the law of the Lord, "a pair of turtledoves, or two young pigeons." Now there was a man in Jerusalem, whose name was Simeon, and this man was righteous and devout, looking for the consolation of Israel, and the Holy Spirit was upon him. And it had been revealed to him by the Holy Spirit that he should not see death before he had seen the Lord's Christ. And inspired by the Spirit he came into the temple; and when the parents brought in the child Jesus, to do for him according to the custom of the law, he took him up in his arms and blessed God and said, "Lord, now lettest thou thy servant depart in peace, according to thy word; for mine eyes have seen thy salvation which thou hast prepared in the presence of all peoples, a light for revelation to the Gentiles, and for glory to thy people Israel."

And his father and his mother marveled at what was said about him; and Simeon blessed them and said to Mary his mother, "Behold, this child is set for the fall and rising of many in Israel, and for a sign that is spoken against (and a sword will pierce through your own soul also), that thoughts out of many hearts may be revealed."

HAIL MARY, full of grace, the Lord is with thee. Blessed art thou among women, and blessed is the fruit of thy womb, Jesus, *whom you presented in the Temple*. Holy Mary, Mother of God, pray for us sinners, now and at the hour of our death. Amen.

REFLECTIONS

- At the Presentation, Mary experiences joy yet glimpses the pain to come. Her response is to maintain her steadfast yes as an act of trust in and obedience to God.

- Trust in God's promises sustained Simeon. Do we cling to God when we don't understand or when answers seem to be slow in coming? Are we obedient in spite of our lack of understanding or even desire?
- "The presentation of Jesus in the temple shows Him to be the firstborn Son who belongs to the Lord" (CCC 529).
- Simeon's faith and desire for God allowed him to recognize Christ.
- Joseph's faithful offering of a pair of turtledoves or two young pigeons was a poor man's alternative to a lamb. When we offer all that we can, God receives it with no less value than an offering that might be greater in the eyes of the world.
- The Holy Family faithfully obeyed the law of Moses as if God had personally given the law. Do we obey the teachings of the Church in the same way, or do we pridefully elevate ourselves above the Wisdom of the ages?
- In this mystery, as in most of the Gospel, Joseph is content to be the quiet protector of Jesus and Mary without desiring any recognition for himself.

CONCLUDING PRAYER

Pray for us, Mary, cause of our joy,
That we may wholeheartedly obey Christ and His Church.

THE FINDING OF THE CHILD JESUS IN THE TEMPLE

After searching for Him for three days, Mary and Joseph find Jesus in the Temple.

FRUIT OF THE MYSTERY: PIETY

SCRIPTURE FOR MEDITATION
LUKE 2:41–52

Now his parents went to Jerusalem every year at the feast of the Passover. And when he was twelve years old, they went up according to custom; and when the feast was ended, as they were returning, the boy Jesus stayed behind in Jerusalem. His parents did not know it, but supposing him to be in the company they went a day's journey, and they sought him among their kinsfolk and acquaintances; and when they did not find him, they returned to Jerusalem, seeking him. After three days they found him in the temple, sitting among the teachers, listening to them and asking them questions; and all who heard him were amazed at his understanding and his answers. And when they saw him they were astonished; and his mother said to him, "Son, why have you treated us so? Behold, your father and I have been looking for you anxiously." And he said to them, "How is it that you sought me? Did you not know that I must be in my Father's house?" And they did not understand the saying which he spoke to them. And he went down with them and came to Nazareth, and was obedient to them; and his mother kept all these things in her heart.

And Jesus increased in wisdom and in stature, and in favor with God and man.

HAIL MARY, full of grace, the Lord is with thee. Blessed art thou among women, and blessed is the fruit of thy womb, Jesus, *whom you found in the Temple*. Holy Mary, Mother of God, pray for us sinners, now and at the hour of our death. Amen.

REFLECTIONS ─────────────────────────

- God promises, "You will seek me and find me; when you seek me with all your heart" (Jer. 29:13). Do we actively and purposefully seek Him daily in all aspects of our lives?

- "Even the closest of human relationships are challenged by the absolute demands of the Kingdom" (*RVM* 20). Are we aware of our call to holiness, and have we embraced it?
- The Holy Family made a pilgrimage to Jerusalem every year. Do we follow this wise pattern of rest and renewal and take our families on pilgrimages to holy places?
- Jesus imparted wisdom to the rabbis in the Temple. He will give us wisdom if we spend time adoring Him in the Blessed Sacrament and engaging Him in prayer through the Scriptures.
- The teachers were impressed with the young Jesus' words. Are we open to being taught by God through faces and circumstances that are unexpected and out of the norm?
- Mary's question is direct, simple, and honest: "Son, why have you treated us so?" (Luke 2:48). Our prayers should likewise be direct, simple, and honest.
- Mary "treasured all these things in her heart" (see Luke 2:51). Do we practice daily mental prayer and reflection on the person and work of Christ?

CONCLUDING PRAYER

Pray for us, Mary, cause of our joy,
That we may will to seek, find, and embrace Jesus in the Mass and in the sacraments.

THE BAPTISM
OF THE LORD

Jesus is baptized by John in the Jordan River.

FRUIT OF THE MYSTERY:
OPENNESS TO THE HOLY SPIRIT

SCRIPTURE FOR MEDITATION
MATTHEW 3:1–2, 11–17

In those days came John the Baptist, preaching in the wilderness of Judea, "Repent, for the kingdom of heaven is at hand.... I baptize you with water for repentance, but he who is coming after me is mightier than I, whose sandals I am not worthy to carry; he will baptize you with the Holy Spirit and with fire. His winnowing fork is in his hand, and he will clear his threshing floor and gather his wheat into the granary, but the chaff he will burn with unquenchable fire."

Then Jesus came from Galilee to the Jordan to John, to be baptized by him. John would have prevented him, saying, "I need to be baptized by you, and do you come to me?" But Jesus answered him, "Let it be so now; for thus it is fitting for us to fulfil all righteousness." Then he consented. And when Jesus was baptized, he went up immediately from the water, and behold, the heavens were opened and he saw the Spirit of God descending like a dove, and alighting on him; and lo, a voice from heaven, saying, "This is my beloved Son, with whom I am well pleased."

HAIL MARY, full of grace, the Lord is with thee. Blessed art thou among women, and blessed is the fruit of thy womb, Jesus, *who was baptized by John.* Holy Mary, Mother of God, pray for us sinners, now and at the hour of our death. Amen.

REFLECTIONS ————————————————————

- "The baptism of Jesus is on his part the humble acceptance and inauguration of his mission as God's suffering Servant" (CCC 536). Are we open to our mission from God? Do we humbly accept it, or do we insist on our way?
- "The Christian must enter into this mystery of humble self-abasement and repentance, go down into the water with Jesus in order to rise with him, [and] be reborn of water and the Spirit so as to become the Father's

beloved son in the Son and 'walk in newness of life'"
(CCC 537; Rom. 6:4).

- With this mystery begins "the revelation of the Kingdom now present in the very person of Jesus" (*RVM* 21).
- As God was pleased with Jesus, so too He is pleased with us when we follow His promptings and avoid quenching the Holy Spirit in our lives.
- For John, only Christ's message mattered, not the world's standards. What are our priorities? Are there people, places, or things that we are more concerned about than our relationship with Him?
- People were attracted to John, despite his appearance, because of his radical fidelity to God. When we are open to the Holy Spirit, He will shine through us and draw others to Himself because of our radical fidelity to Him and His Church.
- Like the ancient Israelites, Jesus passed through water, and then God led Him into the desert. We too must be open to God's redemption and the leading of the Holy Spirit as He works to purify us and prepare us for Heaven.

CONCLUDING PRAYER

Pray for us, Mary, star of the New Evangelization,
That we may be radically faithful to the promptings of the Holy Spirit.

THE WEDDING FEAST AT CANA

Christ changes water into wine at Mary's request.

FRUIT OF THE MYSTERY: MEET-
ING JESUS THROUGH MARY

SCRIPTURE FOR MEDITATION
JOHN 2:1–11

On the third day there was a marriage at Cana in Galilee, and the mother of Jesus was there; Jesus also was invited to the marriage, with his disciples. When the wine failed, the mother of Jesus said to him, "They have no wine." And Jesus said to her, "O woman, what have you to do with me? My hour has not yet come." His mother said to the servants, "Do whatever he tells you." Now six stone jars were standing there, for the Jewish rites of purification, each holding twenty or thirty gallons. Jesus said to them, "Fill the jars with water." And they filled them up to the brim. He said to them, "Now draw some out, and take it to the steward of the feast." So they took it. When the steward of the feast tasted the water now become wine, and did not know where it came from (though the servants who had drawn the water knew), the steward of the feast called the bridegroom and said to him, "Every man serves the good wine first; and when men have drunk freely, then the poor wine; but you have kept the good wine until now." This, the first of his signs, Jesus did at Cana in Galilee, and manifested his glory; and his disciples believed in him.

HAIL MARY, full of grace, the Lord is with thee. Blessed art thou among women, and blessed is the fruit of thy womb, Jesus, *who revealed His glory at your request.* Holy Mary, Mother of God, pray for us sinners, now and at the hour of our death. Amen.

REFLECTIONS ————————————————

- From the beginning, Christ imparts the Faith to His disciples through Mary, "the first among believers."[46]

[46] Saint John Paul II, *Redemptoris Mater*, March 25, 1987, no. 28.

- Jesus chooses this for His first miracle to demonstrate clearly His regard for Mary's petitions and for marriage.
- Mary notices the needs of those around her and commends them to Christ. We can rely on her to do the same for us, and we should do the same for others.
- Through the Rosary, we ask Mary to intercede on our behalf, just as Mary interceded with Jesus at the wedding at Cana.
- Jesus "saves the best for last." As we grow in intimacy with Him, my joy and peace will increase.
- If we bring our needs to Mary, she will take care of them with and through her Son.
- Mary's only directive in Scripture, and the focal point of the entire Rosary, is: "Do whatever He tells you."

CONCLUDING PRAYER

Pray for us, Mary, star of the New Evangelization,
Be our advocate; bring us to Christ.

THE PROCLAMATION OF THE KINGDOM

Christ proclaims the Kingdom of God and calls all to conversion.

FRUIT OF THE MYSTERY: REPENTANCE

SCRIPTURE FOR MEDITATION
MATTHEW 4:17, 23–25

From that time Jesus began to preach, saying, "Repent, for the kingdom of heaven is at hand." And he went about all Galilee, teaching in their synagogues and preaching the gospel of the kingdom and healing every disease and every infirmity among the people. So his fame spread throughout all Syria, and they brought him all the sick, those afflicted with various diseases and pains, demoniacs, epileptics, and paralytics, and he healed them. And great crowds followed him from Galilee and the Decapolis and Jerusalem and Judea and from beyond the Jordan.

HAIL MARY, full of grace, the Lord is with thee. Blessed art thou among women, and blessed is the fruit of thy womb, Jesus, *who preached the Kingdom and forgiveness of sins*. Holy Mary, Mother of God, pray for us sinners, now and at the hour of our death. Amen.

REFLECTIONS

- Jesus invites the brokenhearted and those who have fallen into sin to the Kingdom and "forgives the sins of all who draw near to Him in humble trust" (*RVM* 21).
- Authentic repentance is the fruit of humility. To become a helpless and trusting child in relation to God "is the condition for entering the Kingdom (cf. Matt. 18:3–4). For this, we must humble ourselves and become little" (CCC 526).
- Christ is King of everything: truth, our leisure time, the business world, our families. Do we acknowledge His reign in all areas of our lives?
- We pray, "Thy Kingdom come!" but the next part of the Our Father demands something of us: "Thy will be done." Do we yield to God's will in everything?
- We act as if we were kings: things have to be our way. But Christ's is a Kingdom of service to others, not domination of others.

- "Now is the day of salvation" (2 Cor. 6:2). Are we ready?
- If there are areas of our lives that are not in conformity to His call, in what ways can we specifically turn away from sin and selfishness and turn to God today?

CONCLUDING PRAYER

Pray for us, Mary, star of the New Evangelization,
That we may truly repent and avoid sin and its near occasion.

THE TRANSFIGURATION

Jesus is transfigured on Mount Tabor and becomes radiant.

FRUIT OF THE MYSTERY: DESIRE FOR HOLINESS

SCRIPTURE FOR MEDITATION
MATTHEW 17:1–9

And after six days Jesus took with him Peter and James and John his brother, and led them up a high mountain apart. And he was transfigured before them, and his face shone like the sun, and his garments became white as light. And behold, there appeared to them Moses and Elijah, talking with him. And Peter said to Jesus, "Lord, it is well that we are here; if you wish, I will make three booths here, one for you and one for Moses and one for Elijah." He was still speaking, when lo, a bright cloud overshadowed them, and a voice from the cloud said, "This is my beloved

Son, with whom I am well pleased; listen to him." When the disciples heard this, they fell on their faces, and were filled with awe. But Jesus came and touched them, saying, "Rise, and have no fear." And when they lifted up their eyes, they saw no one but Jesus only.

And as they were coming down the mountain, Jesus commanded them, "Tell no one the vision, until the Son of man is raised from the dead."

HAIL MARY, full of grace, the Lord is with thee. Blessed art thou among women, and blessed is the fruit of thy womb, Jesus, *who was transfigured on Mount Tabor*. Holy Mary, Mother of God, pray for us sinners, now and at the hour of our death. Amen.

REFLECTIONS

- "The glory of the Godhead shines forth from the face of Christ" (*RVM* 21). Contemplating God in Christ is the goal of the Contemplative Rosary.
- "The Transfiguration gives us a foretaste of Christ's glorious coming.... But it also recalls that 'it is through many persecutions that we must enter the Kingdom of God' (Acts 14:22)" (CCC 556).

- Peter sought to stay on Mount Tabor and bask in the glory of the revelation of God. Christ calls him (and us) first to Calvary. We will have plenty of time for Tabor in Heaven.
- "It is good for us" to spend time in prayer contemplating the person and work of Jesus daily.
- Since all the Scriptures point to Christ, meditating on Sacred Scripture is an indispensable way to come to understand Jesus and His mission.
- The three apostles were rewarded for (1) saying yes to Christ's invitation, (2) praying, and (3) staying close to Him.
- The Blessed Trinity provided the apostles with a glimpse of the glory of Jesus' Resurrection in order to give them hope to last through His coming suffering and death. Do we spend time in prayer gazing upon Him in order to allow God to give us the strength and encouragement we need to face the crosses in our own lives?

CONCLUDING PRAYER

Pray for us, Mary, star of the New Evangelization,
That desire for holiness may set our hearts ablaze.

THE INSTITUTION OF THE EUCHARIST

At the Last Supper, Christ changes bread and wine into His Body and Blood.

FRUIT OF THE MYSTERY:
EUCHARISTIC ADORATION

SCRIPTURE FOR MEDITATION
LUKE 22:15–20

And he said to them, "I have earnestly desired to eat this passover with you before I suffer; for I tell you I shall not eat it until it is fulfilled in the kingdom of God." And he took a cup, and when he had given thanks he said, "Take this, and divide it among yourselves; for I tell you that from now on I shall not drink of the fruit of the vine until the kingdom of God comes." And he took bread, and when he had given thanks he broke it and gave it to them, saying, "This is my body which is given for you. Do this in remembrance of me." And likewise the cup after supper, saying, "This cup which is poured out for you is the new covenant in my blood."

> HAIL MARY, full of grace, the Lord is with thee. Blessed art thou among women, and blessed is the fruit of thy womb, Jesus, *who gives Himself to us in the Eucharist.* Holy Mary, Mother of God, pray for us sinners, now and at the hour of our death. Amen.

REFLECTIONS

- In offering His Body and Blood as food and drink, Jesus "testifies 'to the end' his love for humanity, for whose salvation he will offer himself in sacrifice" (*RVM* 21; John 13:1).
- God said, "Let there be light." And there was. Here He says, "This is my Body." And it is.
- If I do not encounter or experience the reality of Christ in the Eucharist, it is likely that I need to change my life: forgive more, serve more, pray more, prepare better for Mass.
- God gives Himself totally to me in the Eucharist. How can I give myself more fully to Him in response? Do I prepare my heart to encounter Him at Mass, or do I

rush in and out as if it is no big deal? Do I spend time distracted or socializing rather than orienting my heart to Him?

- *Eucharist* means "thanksgiving." Am I properly thankful for God's love and forgiveness?
- Adoration of the Blessed Sacrament will increase my love for the Eucharistic Jesus if I will take the time to give myself to Him.
- How can I better prepare myself for receiving this great gift at Mass?

CONCLUDING PRAYER

Pray for us, Mary, star of the New Evangelization,
Help us receive Christ as you did, with reverence and love.

THE AGONY IN THE GARDEN

Jesus prays in Gethsemane on the night before His death.

FRUIT OF THE MYSTERY:
CONFORMITY TO GOD'S WILL

SCRIPTURE FOR MEDITATION
LUKE 22:39–46

And he came out, and went, as was his custom, to the Mount of Olives; and the disciples followed him. And when he came to the place he said to them, "Pray that you may not enter into temptation." And he withdrew from them about a stone's throw, and knelt down and prayed, "Father, if thou art willing, remove this cup from me; nevertheless not my will, but thine, be done." And there appeared to him an angel from heaven, strengthening him. And being in an agony he prayed more earnestly; and his

became like great drops of blood falling down upon
ground. And when he rose from prayer, he came to
the disciples and found them sleeping for sorrow, and he
said to them, "Why do you sleep? Rise and pray that you
may not enter into temptation."

HAIL MARY, full of grace, the Lord is with thee.
Blessed art thou among women, and blessed is the
fruit of thy womb, Jesus, *in agony in the garden for
us* (during Lent: *who suffered agony in the garden for
my sins*). Holy Mary, Mother of God, pray for us
sinners, now and at the hour of our death. Amen.

REFLECTIONS

- In the Garden of Gethsemane, "Jesus encounters all
  the temptations and confronts all the sins of humanity,
  in order to say to the Father: 'Not my will but yours be
  done'" (*RVM* 22; Luke 22:42).
- Jesus' intense agony was rooted in what He knew He
  was about to face—His own brutal torture and execu-
  tion. Like Jesus, though in a much smaller way, we face
  difficult decisions, stress, and pain in our daily lives.
  As we face these trials we can face them with Him,
  knowing that He understands what it means to suffer

and that He will give us the strength to endure and overcome.

- "By accepting in His human will that the Father's will be done, He accepts His death as redemptive" (CCC 612).
- "Could you not stay one hour with me?" Are we too busy to make a holy hour in the presence of the Eucharist for the one who gave all for us?
- "Father, if you are willing ..." It is no shame to pray, and hope, for pain to pass us by, so long as our final prayer is to trust God for the answer that we or others need most.
- Jesus asked His closest friends to pray with Him in His agony. When I am in trouble, others' prayers can support me. Do I comfort Christ in His suffering by comforting those who suffer?
- The disciples disobey Christ's command not because they are wicked, but because they give in to the weakness or draw of their nature. That is often the reason I sin and the reason I need to practice self-denial daily or weekly as a regular spiritual exercise to strengthen me against my weaknesses.

CONCLUDING PRAYER

Pray for us, Mary, Mother of Sorrows,
That we may humbly embrace God's will in all things.

THE SCOURGING AT THE PILLAR

Christ is scourged by the soldiers at Pilate's command.

FRUIT OF THE MYSTERY: MORTIFICATION

Scripture for Meditation
MARK 15:15

So Pilate, wishing to satisfy the crowd, released for them Barabbas; and having scourged Jesus, he delivered him to be crucified.

HAIL MARY, full of grace, the Lord is with thee. Blessed art thou among women, and blessed is the fruit of thy womb, Jesus, *who was scourged for us* (during Lent: *who was scourged for my iniquities*). Holy Mary, Mother of God, pray for us sinners, now and at the hour of our death. Amen.

LECTIONS

"But he was wounded for our transgressions, he was bruised for our iniquities; upon him was the chastisement that made us whole, and with his stripes we are healed" (Isa. 53:5).

- Roman scourges would tear away flesh, and the victim would lose blood, weakening him for crucifixion. The soldiers avoided striking over the heart, to keep the victim alive and thus to maximize his suffering.

- "The Church does not hesitate to impute to Christians the gravest responsibility for the torments inflicted upon Jesus" (CCC 598).

- If He suffered this because of us and for us, there is nothing we should ever refuse to do for Him.

- In imitation of Christ, we must offer ourselves to God and entrust all that we are to Him, even if that means suffering, especially suffering on behalf of others and the suffering that comes when we say no to self and yes to God and the needs of others.

- Now the cost of Christ's faithfulness to His Father's will is made manifest (see *RVM* 22).

- In the garden, Heaven's help was obvious—an angel. In the scourging, the interior grace of hope is Christ's only help. We can expect the same when we give ourselves to God and offer up our pain for others ⸱ the midst of our suffering.

CONCLUDING PRAYER ─────────────

Pray for us, Mary, Mother of Sorrows,
That we may accept sufferings and setbacks out of love for Christ.

THE CROWNING WITH THORNS

The soldiers weave a crown of thorns and press it onto Christ's head.

FRUIT OF THE MYSTERY: MORAL COURAGE

SCRIPTURE FOR MEDITATION
MATTHEW 27:28–30; JOHN 19:4–6

And they stripped him and put a scarlet robe upon him, and plaiting a crown of thorns they put it on his head, and put a reed in his right hand. And kneeling before him they mocked him, saying, "Hail, King of the Jews!" And they spat upon him, and took the reed and struck him on the head.

Pilate went out again, and said to them, "Behold, I am bringing him out to you, that you may know that I find no crime in him." So Jesus came out, wearing the crown of thorns and the purple robe. Pilate said to them, "Here the man!" When the chief priests and the officers saw him, they cried out, "Crucify him, crucify him!" Pilate said to them, "Take him yourselves and crucify him, for I find no crime in him."

> HAIL MARY, full of grace, the Lord is with thee. Blessed art thou among women, and blessed is the fruit of thy womb, Jesus, *who was crowned with thorns for us* (during Lent: *who was mocked and crowned with thorns because of my transgressions*). Holy Mary, Mother of God, pray for us sinners, now and at the hour of our death. Amen.

REFLECTIONS

- "*Ecce homo!* This abject suffering reveals not only the love of God but also the meaning of man himself" (*RVM* 22).
- We too must accept suffering that comes when we authentically and unequivocally identify ourselves with Christ before the world.
- "There is not, never has been, and never will be a single human being for whom Christ did not suffer" (CCC 605).[47] This includes those we most dislike or despise.

[47] Quoting Council of Quiercy (853): DS 624; cf. 2 Cor. 5:15; 1 John 2:2.

- We might avoid evangelizing out of fear of ridicule. But without risking ridicule, we will never fully imitate Christ.
- Even the Rosary can be an empty crown if we merely "say" it instead of pray it.
- My sincere adoration of Jesus as I pray the Rosary combats the mockery of the Roman soldiers.
- Jesus' suffering can purify my heart and my thoughts and grant me "the mind of Christ" (1 Cor. 2:16).

CONCLUDING PRAYER

Pray for us, Mary, Mother of Sorrows,
That we may witness to the Gospel, even at cost to ourselves.

THE CARRYING OF THE CROSS

Jesus Carries His Heavy Cross to Calvary.

FRUIT OF THE MYSTERY· PATIENCE

Scripture for Meditation
JOHN 19:17; LUKE 23:26

So they took Jesus, and he went out, bearing his own cross.

And as they led him away, they seized one Simon of Cyrene, who was coming in from the country, and laid on him the cross, to carry it behind Jesus.

HAIL MARY, full of grace, the Lord is with thee. Blessed art thou among women, and blessed is the fruit of thy womb, Jesus, *who embraced His Cross for us* (during Lent: *who embraced the Cross because of my sins*). Holy Mary, Mother of God, pray for us sinners, now and at the hour of our death. Amen.

"The meaning, origin and fulfillment of man is to be found in Christ, the God who humbles himself out of love 'even until death, death on a cross'" (*RVM* 22; Phil. 2:8). Jesus was ridiculed, tortured, and crucified for us. He understands the plight of the abused, oppressed, and all those who suffer at the hands of others.

- Christ accepted His heavy Cross without professing His innocence, because He was carrying it for the guilty—for us.

- In His suffering, Christ is surrounded not by throngs of those who love Him, but instead by those who hate and mock Him. Although He has the power to stop it all and bring all to justice, He patiently endures His torture so that we might be redeemed.

- The cross I have been given has been hand-tested by Christ so that it will be neither too heavy nor too light.

- The Blessed Mother was close by when her Son was suffering. She is also close by when we, her other children, suffer.

- Are we sick of trying to be holy and always failing? Our struggle for holiness, with all of its stumbling and fumbling, is our lifelong way of the cross. We need not despair, but we must get up and keep trying and ask Christ, the exemplar of patience, to help us to be patient in our trials.

CONCLUDING PRAYER——————————————

Pray for us, Mary, Mother of Sorrows,
That we may practice patience with ourselves and with others.

THE CRUCIFIXION

Jesus is nailed to the Cross and dies.

FRUIT OF THE MYSTERY: SALVATION

SCRIPTURE FOR MEDITATION
JOHN 19:23–30

When the soldiers had crucified Jesus they took his garments and made four parts, one for each soldier; also his tunic. But the tunic was without seam, woven from top to bottom; so they said to one another, "Let us not tear it, but cast lots for it to see whose it shall be." This was to fulfil the scripture, "They parted my garments among them, and for my clothing they cast lots." So the soldiers did this. But standing by the cross of Jesus were his mother, and his mother's sister, Mary the wife of Clopas, and Mary Magdalene. When Jesus saw his mother, and the disciple whom he loved standing near, he said to his mother, "Woman, behold, your son!" Then he said to the disciple, "Behold, ɔur mother!" And from that hour the disciple took her to his own home.

After this Jesus, knowing that all was now finished, said (to fulfil the scripture), "I thirst." A bowl full of vinegar stood there; so they put a sponge full of the vinegar on hyssop and held it to his mouth. When Jesus had received the vinegar, he said, "It is finished"; and he bowed his head and gave up his spirit.

HAIL MARY, full of grace, the Lord is with thee. Blessed art thou among women, and blessed is the fruit of thy womb, Jesus, *who was crucified for us* (during Lent: *who was crucified because of my sins*). Holy Mary, Mother of God, pray for us sinners, now and at the hour of our death. Amen.

REFLECTIONS

- "The sorrowful mysteries help the believer to relive the death of Jesus, to stand at the foot of the Cross beside Mary, to enter with her into the depths of God's love for man and to experience all its life-giving power" (*RVM* 22).
- "On the cross, Jesus became sin personified that we may never be afraid to come to Him Who never will reject

us. He has suffered everything we suffer and He is closest to those who feel the most sinful and the farthest away, for they are the ones who resemble Him the most when He was alone and abandoned on the cross."[48]

- "It is love 'to the end' (John 13:1) that confers on Christ's sacrifice, its value as redemption and reparation, as atonement and satisfaction" (CCC 616).

- Christ died for the very people who were mocking Him, blaspheming Him, and killing Him. He created those whom He knew would torture and reject Him. His love transcends His suffering and discomfort. Do we love in a way that endures suffering and betrayal?

- "Apart from the Cross there is no other ladder by which we may get to heaven" (CCC 618).[49]

- "Since our sins made the Lord Christ suffer the torment of the cross, those who plunge themselves into disorders and crimes crucify the Son of God anew" (CCC 598).[50]

---

[48] Fr. Martin Lucia, SS. CC., *Rosary Meditations from Mother Teresa of Calcutta: Loving Jesus with the Heart of Mary* (Missionaries of the Blessed Sacrament, 1984).

[49] Quoting St. Rose of Lima; cf. P. Hansen, *Vita mirabilis* (Louvain, 1668).

[50] Quoting *Roman Catechism* I, 5, 11; cf. Heb. 6:6; 1 Cor. 2:8.

- "The Church, following the apostles, teaches that Christ died for all men without exception" (CCC 605). Do we offer His love to all, so that His death for them will not be in vain?

Concluding Prayer

Pray for us, Mary, Mother of Sorrows,
That Christ's death on the Cross may save us from sin and condemnation.

THE RESURRECTION

Three days after His death, Jesus rises, glorious and immortal.

FRUIT OF THE MYSTERY: FAITH

SCRIPTURE FOR MEDITATION
MATTHEW 28:1-10

Now after the sabbath, toward the dawn of the first day of the week, Mary Magdalene and the other Mary went to see the sepulchre. And behold, there was a great earthquake; for an angel of the Lord descended from heaven and came and rolled back the stone, and sat upon it. His appearance was like lightning, and his raiment white as snow. And for fear of him the guards trembled and became like dead men. But the angel said to the women, "Do not be afraid; for I know that you seek Jesus who was crucified. He is not here; for he has risen, as he said. Come, see the place where he lay. Then go quickly and tell his disciples that he has risen from the dead, and behold, he is going before you to Galilee; there you will see him. Lo, I have told you." So they departed quickly from the tomb with fear and great joy, and ran to tell his disciples. And behold, Jesus met them and said, "Hail!" And they came up and took hold of his feet and worshiped him. Then Jesus said to them, "Do not be afraid; go and tell my brethren to go to Galilee, and there they will see me."

HAIL MARY, full of grace, the Lord is with thee. Blessed art thou among women, and blessed is the fruit of thy womb, Jesus, *who is risen from the dead.* Holy Mary, Mother of God, pray for us sinners, now and at the hour of our death. Amen.

REFLECTIONS

- "Contemplating the Risen One, Christians *rediscover the reasons for their own faith* and relive the joy not only of those to whom Christ appeared ... *but also the joy of Mary*" (*RVM* 23).
- "The joy of the risen Christ is greater than pain. The hope that comes from His resurrection is the victory over our own fear of suffering and death. We follow Jesus; follow His steps through this world and into the next" (*Gold Book of Prayers*).

- Christ's Resurrection is a real event that was historically verified (see CCC 639).
- Do we think of the Resurrection as a fairy tale? If it isn't literally true, then Christianity is wicked—the Cross without redemption.
- The women who visited the tomb were so filled with joy that they ran to tell the others. Is our encounter with Christ so real that we can't help but tell anyone who will listen?
- The Roman soldiers witnessed the Resurrection without being changed by it. Are we allowing the Resurrection to change us, or are we resisting God's will and thus dulled to the reality of His presence, power, and redemption?
- Sunday is the feast of the Resurrection, the Lord's Day—the only day set aside for Him and for holy rest and rejoicing. How do we make it holy in our lives?

CONCLUDING PRAYER —————

Pray for us, Mary, gate of Heaven,
That faith in the risen Christ may permeate our lives.

THE ASCENSION

Jesus ascends into Heaven forty days after His Resurrection.

FRUIT OF THE MYSTERY: HOPE

SCRIPTURE FOR MEDITATION
ACTS 1:6–11

So when they had come together, they asked him, "Lord, will you at this time restore the kingdom to Israel?" He said to them, "It is not for you to know times or seasons which the Father has fixed by his own authority. But you shall receive power when the Holy Spirit has come upon you; and you shall be my witnesses in Jerusalem and in all Judea and Samaria and to the end of the earth." And when he had said this, as they were looking on, he was lifted up, and a cloud took him out of their sight. And while they were gazing into heaven as he went, behold, two men stood by them in white robes, and said, "Men of Galilee, why do you stand looking into heaven? This Jesus, who was taken up from you into heaven, will come in the same way as you saw him go into heaven."

HAIL MARY, full of grace, the Lord is with thee. Blessed art thou among women, and blessed is the fruit of thy womb, Jesus, *who ascended into Heaven*. Holy Mary, Mother of God, pray for us sinners, now and at the hour of our death. Amen.

REFLECTIONS ——————————————————————

- "Set your minds on things that are above, not on things that are on earth. For you have died, and your life is hid with Christ in God. When Christ who is our life appears, then you also will appear with him in glory" (Col. 3:2–4).
- "In this day and age unless Christians are revolutionaries they are not Christians. They must be revolutionaries through grace!"[51] We must not be complacent. We must speak up and ask hard questions. We must love difficult people. We must pray and give until it hurts. We are already part of a revolutionary movement that has been

[51] Pope Francis, Address to participants in the ecclesial convention of the Diocese of Rome, June 17, 2013.

sweeping the world for more than two thousand years. People around the globe are martyred every day for their Christian Faith. What are we willing to do for ours?

- We can imagine that Mary would have told the Apostles to "do whatever He tells you" after Jesus' Ascension, when she joined them in awaiting the Holy Spirit (see RVM 14). Do we heed her guidance?

- Before the Ascension, Christ was to be found on earth, always confined to one place; now we can find Him and encounter Him anywhere we are.

- By telling the apostles to convert the nations and then departing, Christ made His message clear: we are to do His work now.

- We have faith, even though Christ is covered in clouds. We have hope, because we know all authority is His. We have love, because He has entrusted us with so much.

- Christ will return in the same way and without warning (Acts 1:11). Are we ready for His return? Do we regularly pursue holiness and participate in the sacrament of reconciliation?

CONCLUDING PRAYER

Pray for us, Mary, gate of Heaven,
That we may cling to and live in our hope of God's faithfulness.

THE DESCENT OF THE HOLY SPIRIT

The Holy Spirit descends upon Mary and the apostles.

FRUIT OF THE MYSTERY: WISDOM

SCRIPTURE FOR MEDITATION
ACTS 2:1–4

When the day of Pentecost had come, they were all to-gether in one place. And suddenly a sound came from heaven like the rush of a mighty wind, and it filled all the house where they were sitting. And there appeared to them tongues as of fire, distributed and resting on each one of them. And they were all filled with the Holy Spirit and began to speak in other tongues, as the Spirit gave them utterance.

HAIL MARY, full of grace, the Lord is with thee. Blessed art thou among women, and blessed is the fruit of thy womb, Jesus, *pouring forth His Holy Spirit.* Holy Mary, Mother of God, pray for us sinners, now and at the hour of our death. Amen.

REFLECTIONS ───────────────────────

- Pentecost "reveals the face of the Church as a family gathered together with Mary, enlivened by the powerful outpouring of the Spirit and ready for the mission of evangelization" (*RVM* 23).
- "Through the Holy Spirit we are restored to paradise, led back to the Kingdom of heaven and adopted as children, given confidence to call God 'Father' and to share in Christ's grace, called children of light and given a share in eternal glory" (CCC 736).[52]
- "On that day [Pentecost], the Holy Trinity is fully revealed" (CCC 732).
- "By His coming, which never ceases, the Holy Spirit causes the world to enter into the 'last days', the time of the Church" (CCC 732).

[52] Quoting Saint Basil, *De Spiritu Sancto*, 15, 36: PG 32,132.

- The Bible says that only a small portion of Christ's teaching is contained within its pages (see John 21:25). The rest is given to the Church by the Holy Spirit and through the Magisterium.
- "The fruit of the Spirit is love, joy, peace, patience, kindness, goodness, faithfulness, gentleness, self-control" (Gal. 5:22–23). Are these fruits normative in our lives? Would others describe us as persons of love, joy, peace, patience, and so forth? If not, why not?
- The Holy Spirit turned the cowardly apostles into world conquerors. He will transform us, too, if we will say yes and embrace His calling in our lives.

CONCLUDING PRAYER

Pray for us, Mary, gate of Heaven,
That the Holy Spirit will fill us with wisdom and power to do His will.

THE ASSUMPTION OF MARY

At the end of her life, Mary is taken body and soul into Heaven and is united with her Divine Son.

FRUIT OF THE MYSTERY: DEVOTION TO MARY

SCRIPTURE FOR MEDITATION
REVELATION 12:1–6

And a great portent appeared in heaven, a woman clothed with the sun, with the moon under her feet, and on her head a crown of twelve stars; she was with child and she cried out in her pangs of birth, in anguish for delivery. And another portent appeared in heaven; behold, a great red dragon, with seven heads and ten horns, and seven diadems upon his heads. His tail swept down a third of the stars of heaven, and cast them to the earth. And the dragon stood before the woman who was about to bear a child, that he might devour her child when she brought it forth; she brought forth a male child, one who is to rule all the nations with a rod of iron, but her child was caught up to God and to his throne, and the woman fled into the wilderness, where she has a place prepared by God, in which to be nourished for one thousand two hundred and sixty days.

HAIL MARY, full of grace, the Lord is with thee. Blessed art thou among women, and blessed is the fruit of thy womb, Jesus, *who assumed you into Heaven*. Holy Mary, Mother of God, pray for us sinners, now and at the hour of our death. Amen.

REFLECTIONS

- In Heaven, Mary "already shares in the glory of her Son's Resurrection, anticipating the resurrection of all members of his Body" (CCC 974).
- Mary was, "from the first moment of Her conception, by a singular grace and privilege of almighty God and by virtue of the merits of Jesus Christ, savior of the human race, preserved immune from all stain of original sin" (CCC 491).[53]

[53] Quoting Pius IX, *Ineffabilis Deus* (1854): DS 2803.

- "To become the Mother of the Savior, Mary 'was enriched by God with gifts appropriate to such a role (CCC 490).[54]
- "It was fitting that she, who had kept her virginity in childbirth, should keep her own body free from all corruption even after death."[55]
- Mary "shines forth on earth until the day of the Lord shall come, a sign of certain hope and comfort to the pilgrim People of God" (CCC 972).[56]
- Since Mary is at her Son's side in Heaven, her prayers are powerful to aid us.
- Like Adam, Eve was banished from the Garden of Eden because of disobedience. Like Jesus, Mary was welcomed into Heaven because of obedience.

CONCLUDING PRAYER —————————————

Pray for us, Mary, gate of Heaven,
That we may contemplate Christ with you and in you.

---

[54] Quoting Second Vatican Council, Dogmatic Constitution on the Church *Lumen Gentium*, November 21, 1964, no. 56.

[55] Pope Pius XII, *Munificentissimus Deus* no. 21, quoting Saint John Damascene.

[56] Quoting *Lumen Gentium* 68; cf. 2 Pet. 3:10.

THE CORONATION OF MARY

**Mary is gloriously crowned
Queen of Heaven and Earth.**

FRUIT OF THE MYSTERY: ETERNAL HAPPINESS

SCRIPTURE FOR MEDITATION
PSALM 45:6–11

Your divine throne endures for ever and ever. Your royal scepter is a scepter of equity; you love righteousness and hate wickedness. Therefore God, your God, has anointed you with the oil of gladness above your fellows; your robes are all fragrant with myrrh and aloes and cassia. From ivory palaces stringed instruments make you glad; daughters of kings are among your ladies of honor; at your right hand stands the queen in gold of Ophir.

Hear, O daughter, consider, and incline your ear; forget your people and your father's house; and the king will desire your beauty. Since he is your lord, bow to him.

HAIL MARY, full of grace, the Lord is with thee. Blessed art thou among women, and blessed is the fruit of thy womb, Jesus, *who crowned you Queen of Heaven and Earth*. Holy Mary, Mother of God, pray for us sinners, now and at the hour of our death. Amen.

REFLECTIONS

- "Mary shines forth as Queen of the Angels and Saints, the anticipation and the supreme realization of the eschatological state of the Church" (*RVM* 23).
- "Hail, O Queen of Heaven and earth, to whose empire everything is subject which is under God. Hail, O sure refuge of sinners, whose mercy fails no one."[57]
- Mary said to St. Faustina, "I am not only the Queen of Heaven, but also the Mother of Mercy, and your Mother."[58]
- "We believe that the Holy Mother of God, the new Eve, Mother of the Church, continues in Heaven to

---

[57] Saint Louis de Montfort, "Act of Total Consecration to Mary," *True Devotion to Mary*.
[58] *Diary of St. M. Faustina Kowalska* (Stockbridge: Marians of the Immaculate Conception, 1996), no. 330.

exercise Her maternal role on behalf of the members of Christ."[59]

- If Mary is our queen, she is queen of all aspects of our lives; not just our religious lives, but our social lives, work lives, home lives, and interior lives as well.
- Mary is forever blessed, for she heard the word of God, said yes to it, and lived it (see Luke 11:28). Do we do the same?
- "Be intent on the things above rather than on earth, for here we have no lasting dwelling place. We have our citizenship in Heaven."[60]

CONCLUDING PRAYER

Pray for us, Mary, gate of Heaven,
Lead us to the Beatific Vision.

---

[59] Blessed Paul VI, Apostolic Letter *Solemni Hac Liturgia* (Credo of the People of God), June 30, 1968, no. 15.
[60] *Rosary Meditations from Mother Teresa.*

The Fifteen Promises of Mary to Christians Who Recite the Rosary

(Given to Saint Dominic and Blessed Alan de la Roche)

1. Whoever shall faithfully serve me by the recitation of the Rosary shall receive signal graces.

2. I promise my special protection and the greatest graces to all those who shall recite the Rosary.

3. The Rosary shall be a powerful armor against Hell; it will destroy vice, decrease sin, and defeat heresies.

4. It will cause virtue and good works to flourish; it will obtain for souls the abundant mercy of God; it will withdraw the hearts of men from the love of the world and its vanities, and will lift them to the desire of eternal things. Oh, that souls would sanctify themselves by this means.

5. The soul that recommends itself to me by the recitation of the Rosary shall not perish.

6. Whoever shall recite the Rosary devoutly, applying himself to the consideration of its sacred mysteries, shall never be conquered by misfortune. God will not chastise him in His justice; he shall not perish by an unprovided death; if he be just, he shall remain in the grace of God, and become worthy of eternal life.

7. Whoever shall have a true devotion for the Rosary shall not die without the sacraments of the Church.

8. Those who are faithful to reciting the Rosary shall have during their life and at their death the light of God and the plentitude of His graces; at the moment of death they shall participate in the merits of the saints in paradise.

9. I shall deliver from purgatory those who have been devoted to the Rosary.

10. The faithful children of the Rosary shall merit a high degree of glory in Heaven.

11. You shall obtain all you ask of me by recitation of the Rosary.

12. All those who propagate the Holy Rosary shall be aided by me in their necessities.

13. I have obtained from my Divine Son that all the advocates of the Rosary shall have for intercessors the

entire Celestial Court during their life and at the hour of death.

14. All who recite the Rosary are my sons, and brothers of my only Son, Jesus Christ.

15. Devotion of my Rosary is a great sign of predestination.[61]

---

[61] Imprimatur: + Patrick J. Hayes, D.D., Archbishop of New York.

Titles of Artworks
All images are in the public domain.

JOYFUL MYSTERIES

The Annunciation by Bartolomé Murrillo, Wikimedia Commons
Visitación by Juan del Castillo, Wikimedia Commons
The Adoration of the Shepherds by Bartolomé Murillo, Wikipedia
Saint Simeon with the Christ Child by Jusepe de Ribera, Wikimedia
    Commons
Jesus among the Doctors by Jusepe de Ribera, Wikimedia Commons

LUMINOUS MYSTERIES

Baptism of Christ by Bartolomé Murillo, Wikiart
The Marriage Feast at Cana by Bartolomé Murillo, Wikiart
Christ at the Pool of Bethesda by Bartolomé Murillo, Wikiart
Transfiguration of Christ by Paolo Veronese, Wikimedia Commons
The Last Supper by Juan Ribalta, Wikimedia Commons

SORROWFUL MYSTERIES

Jesús en el Huerto de Getsemaní by Andrea Vaccaro, Wikimedia Commons
Christ After the Flagellation Contemplated by a Christian Soul by Diego
    Velazquez, Wikiart
Ecce Homo by Murillo, Wikimedia Commons
Christ Meets the Virgin on the Way to Calvary by Bartolomé Murillo,
    Wikimedia Commons
Christ Crucified by Diego Velazquez, Wikimedia Commons

GLORIOUS MYSTERIES

Resurrección del Señor by Bartolomé Murillo, Wikimedia Commons
Ascensión del Señor by Antonio de Lanchares, Wikimedia Commons
Pentecostés by Juan Bautista Mayno, Wikipedia
The Assumption of the Virgin by Bartolomé Murillo, Wikiart
Coronation of the Virgin by Velazquez, Wikiart